Incarcerated Soul

Whispers of an Estranged Heart

Sneha Shukla

BookLeaf Publishing

India | USA | UK

Made with ❤ on the BookLeaf Publishing Platform
www.bookleafpub.in
www.bookleafpub.com

Dedication

For every heart that's too kind for this world,
For the hearts that never stop loving,
For those who give without expecting, and still find a
way to keep giving.

A special dedication to the one I call home,
For your unwavering belief, and your constant support.
You've been my anchor and my strength.
To my friends, who stood by me through thick and thin,
Who helped me bare my soul,
And for the love and laughter that kept me going
through the toughest times.

And to my doting and wonderfully crazy family - thank
you.
You are the roots that ground me, and the wings that lift
me.

With all my love,
This one's for you.

Preface

I bare my soul here to the reverie and pain I've danced with most of my nights…

Incarcerated Soul: Whispers of an Estranged Heart is a collection born from the quietest hours of the night, where thoughts become louder than the world around them. It is a journey through the raw and fragile parts of the self, captured in verses that sought refuge in the silence of darkness. These poems are not simply words on paper; they are the echoes of a soul searching for understanding, for release, for connection.

Writing in the stillness of the night became my sanctuary, where I could confront the parts of me that felt imprisoned - by my own fears, my own doubts, my own unspoken truths. Each poem reflects an attempt to unravel those knots, to free myself from the chains I had unknowingly wrapped around my heart. In the quiet solitude, my thoughts spilled onto the page, transforming the weight of my emotions into something tangible. The title, *Incarcerated Soul*, speaks to the isolation we often face within ourselves—when our own minds become prisons and our hearts feel estranged, unable to reach the world around them. These poems are whispers from that estranged heart, yearning to be understood, yearning for release.

This collection is not just mine. It is for anyone who has ever felt the walls closing in on them, for anyone who has experienced the haunting quiet of loneliness, or the silent battles fought within. In these pages, you may find fragments of your own soul, a reflection of the quiet struggles that often go unseen.

I offer this book as both a confession and a release, a tribute to the power of words to heal, to free, and to connect us across the distances of our own hearts. May these whispers find their way to yours.

Acknowledgements

To the one i call home whose belief in me has been the quiet spark behind every word written here—*thank you.* You are the reason and the source, I found the courage to trust my voice and the strength to begin. Your unwavering support has been my foundation, and your faith in me has made all the difference. In your quiet strength, I found the courage to write.

To my family—Mom, Dad, and my brother—your love, wisdom, and unwavering support have shaped who I am. Every word I write carries the strength and resilience I've inherited from you.

To my brother, whose steady presence and belief in me have given me wings when I needed them most—*thank you* for lifting me higher and encouraging me to soar.

To my younger sister, who has been my constant listener —*thank you* for always being there, for your unwavering support, and for giving me a safe space to express my fears, doubts, and hopes. Your kind heart has been a source of strength I will never take for granted.

To my best friends—*thank you* for showing up during the darkest moments, for your quiet encouragement and the comfort of knowing I am never alone. Your love has carried me through this journey, and I am endlessly grateful for your presence in my life.

To the music that allowed me to lose myself in my thoughts, to the notes that became the backdrop for my words, and to the quiet corner of my study where ideas blossomed in solitude—*thank you* for giving me the space to create.

And most of all, **to the painful nights** when sadness could no longer be contained—*thank you*. It is in the rawest, most vulnerable moments that my creativity was born. I acknowledge that *it is through the pain, the quiet suffering, and the moments of being lost that I found the most beautiful, honest parts of myself.* It is in those dark hours, when all seemed impossible, that my truest creativity came to life. *Without that pain, there would be no voice, no expression, no release.* Through these struggles, I have learned that sometimes the most beautiful things in life come from the deepest of wounds.

This book is a testament to all of you, to the pain that shaped it, and to the love that made it possible. *I am forever grateful for every person who has walked beside me on this journey.* With all my heart, I thank you.

1. "Beneath the Waves of Her Being"

Depth of an ocean
Footloose and fancy-free, she is
Constrained within the boundaries of an imbecilic
society,
With a zestful, enlightened soul,
Living her death with each passing second, enduring
dream of the others,
Confining herself in the darkness, dwindling deeper
down.
Blind to the witching hour of her breath,
This world grooves on the cadence of her tears,
serenading every agony,
Procuring in the darkest and most hideous corners of her
soul.
She longs to be set free to live,
To surrender to her dreams,
To voice her misery,
To truly feel herself
She's lost in the midst of atrocious anticipations.

The forebearer who gifted her life has marked her with excruciating, abysmal pain.
Little did she hope, and she continues to hope...
scintillating soul that she is.
For a companion,
One who will take her hand, guiding her to strike the wavering beam of light,
Finally discerning the animus of her life.
And there she is,
Not meant to be celestial at dusk... living her life in oblivion.
Camouflaging... in oceanic waves that she is!
She is life!

2. "Whispers of Tenderness"

In the past few weeks,
a new era of healing has unfolded before me.
A handful of days,
delicate and transformative, have elevated moments of
comfort, affection, and redemption.
Forever the embodiment of clumsiness and imperfection,
What appears beautiful and regal is but a fleeting
illusion, a fragile facade.
Through years of a life locked away in silence,
With buried sentiments and a fractured heart,
I surrendered to the numbing cloak of solitude.
But then,
I was unraveled by a cloak of warmth and fleeting,
crushing bear hugs
Thoughts drifting like whispers,
from deep contemplation to walking hand in hand
through sacred halls,
Wrapped in tender serenity, bathed in peace.
Besotted by the moments of soothing embrace, the soft,
doting kisses on my forehead,

It was a slice of heaven made real,
a world of comfort so tender.
Every gentle touch, every caress, sent a shiver of quiet
affection
A longing that had been woven through the years, now
softly unfolding in the light.

3. "When the Moon Weaves Dreams of the Sun"

It was a day of many firsts,

A moment when everything felt new,

Wrapped in the tightest embrace,

As though time itself slowed down,

A roaring, energized surge toward the summit,

The start of something endless,

With dance moves that were rarely seen

Fleeting, like whispers of joy in the wind.

Hand in hand, we ventured through the chilly winds,

His warmth a contrast to the cold,

And there it was—

A euphoric reach to the crest,

Where the world stretched wide beneath us,

A heart full of ecstasy,

And the nostalgic love of something older, something

deeper.

She, the girl who had lived in the quiet embrace of dusk,

Who had danced with the moonlight,
Found solace in the shadows,
Her heart echoing with the gentle glow of the stars,
In her world, the moon was always enough.
But now, somehow
Her soul, once bound to the pale silver of the night,
Had inexplicably fallen in love with the sun,
With the warm, bold light of day,
Its golden rays calling to her,
Pulling her from the darkness she had known,
To bask in the warmth she had once feared.
He, the boy who had always been in love with the sun,
Who had lived for its rise,
Its radiance fueling his every step,
Now stood beside her
A bridge between the light and the dark.
He who had long adored the sun's fiery brilliance,
Had discovered, in her, a new light,
A new warmth he had never known,
And in her eyes, the moonlight still flickered,
A soft glow that reminded him
The sun's warmth is only truly felt when the night gives
way.
And there, amidst the golden embrace of dawn,
The girl who had once loved the moon
Found herself bathed in the sun's light,
Her heart blossoming,

No longer afraid of the brightness,
For she had learned that the sun and the moon
Though different,
Could coexist,
Each beautiful in its own way,
Each lighting up the world in its own time.
The magnificence of those golden rays
A love that had once seemed impossible,
Now lighting up her heart,
Filling their world with warmth and endless possibility.

4. "Echoes of a Shattered Soul"

Drowning in the dry land of anxieties,
In the realm of panic attacks,
What happens to the unconditional promises?
What happens to forever?
How do I explain the chaos inside?
Scream the truth or look past it?
Do I escape to the land of silence,
Just so I can breathe?
Carrying the pain of a lifetime,
The weight of unseen battles too heavy to bear.
Shattered heart aches louder than hope,
Fearful of the past,
Scars overshadowing the present.
I stand by the fight, entangled in the momentary chaos,
And
Life mocks again.
A fresh breath of air,
Suffocating the remains,
For what's left.

I scream into the void,
Surrounded by deaf ears,
Opening up my soul
To feel all over again—
A loving soul full of rage,
Waiting to be burnt alive.

5. "Empty Star"

There it stood,
Tapping gently on the shattered doors of my fractured
heart,
A heart I had long battled with,
Clutched tight,
Bound together by sorrow and hollow emptiness.
Once more, it unraveled, destined to be shattered anew,
Or perhaps it was time to be healed -once and for all.
So, this is what it feels like?
I thought I had outgrown it.
I had adhered to every rule that ever was,
And yet, how did this come to be?
Slipping into the abyss,
Love that destroys, enrapturing my very soul,
Suddenly, it became all too real.
Love that tangled life in its own web,
A crippling ache, rendering me almost helpless,
Shuddering with every realization sinking deeper.
Did I fall in love once more?
Why does it all feel so unfamiliar?

Years spent in exile, fleeing from vulnerability,
Now, it's all too tangible.
Scattering the fragments of my heart, strewn across the
floor.
There I stood, left hollow,
With a void that no force could ever fill.

6. "Falling into Forever"

Day that i resented for fleeting years
Evoking pain of my every being
I found diversion in the arms of nature
It morphed into something real!
This was a just another escape to my world
Little did i know,
Destiny had its own course of magic set into play
Hitting the trail
We caught glimpses of the edges
of possible parallel world
and
The day closed, unfolding into the most unforgettable
night.
A bit of rest and waking up to dotting forehead kisses
pulled into the night of magic
Perched on his lap beneath a sky brimming with
galaxies,
His arms wrapped around me, a perfect embrace.
We watched the stars shimmer, a cosmic dance,
Counting their brilliance as if time stood still.

In that moment, I reveled in the nostalgia,
For this was the dream I had always held
The most romantic, magical night I'd ever imagined.
Finally, drifting into sleep with heartiest laughter,
And quiet moments of profound realization,
A yearning to relive this over and over again.
Two introverts, fragile and fearful,
Falling into love—timid yet all-encompassing,
Like stars hidden behind the veil of the night,
Their quiet glow burning, silently eternal.

7. "Strength in Tenderness"

I grew up believing kindness and emotion were
weaknesses,
shaped by the world that surrounded me.
I wove the illusion of a girl who cared for little
For criticism, for disrespect, for everything that chipped
away
at her fragile confidence, piece by piece.
I bottled up emotions for decades, unaware
That in the process, I would lose myself.
There is nothing more excruciating than forgetting who
you once were,
Than not recalling what that innocent girl felt like.
It was in this moment that I laughed until tears streamed
down,
Only for reality to come crashing with cruel force.
I no longer possess those breathless, carefree laughs,
Nor the smile that once warmed my soul,
As now, all feels like a mask.
I no longer dance alone in my room,
I no longer know the hue that lights up my heart,

What stirs joy in my chest,
Or what I would do when in need of solitude.
Half my life has slipped by,
And I still don't know how to say no.
That's when it clicked
Is this really weakness?
How hard it must be to wear your heart upon your
sleeve,
To smile with eyes burdened by unshed tears,
To act as if you're fine, so others won't hurt,
To put others before yourself, even when drowning in
your own battles,
To answer late-night calls, talking someone out of
despair,
While struggling to catch your own breath.
What kind of strength does it take
To love with such intensity, to care so deeply,
Even with a heart fractured into pieces?
To everyone who has been taught otherwise,
You are not alone,
And there is nothing weak about being the purest, most
giving soul in a world so cruel and selfish.
It is because of you that this world still has reason to
exist.

8. "A Touch I Dread, A Touch I Crave"

Touch

It was a word I never truly understood,
A sensation I feared my entire life
Running from the very warmth I now ache for.
Yet here I am,
Yearning for it with a desperate longing,
A longing so deep it pulls at my soul,
For a touch that sparks life in every corner of my being,
A touch that makes me feel truly alive.
The only kind of touch I ever dreamed of,
Since the moment I became aware of this world,
Was a hug
To be held so tightly
That the shattered pieces of me might find their way
back together,
To be embraced so fiercely
That I would fall apart,
Tear down the walls I spent so long building.
Then one night,

Like a soft breath of air,
It arrived.
With the innocence of a child,
Slowly, tenderly,
Drawing me into an embrace
So gentle,
So warm,
So full of love,
I froze in disbelief,
A moment of shock before I surrendered
Melting in the purity of what I was being given.
We spent the night like this,
Locked in a hug that swung between comfort and
release,
My face buried in the curve of his neck,
A tear slipping silently down my cheek.
Every breath he took brushing against my skin,
A steady rhythm,
As the years of bottled emotions,
Of pretending to be strong,
Finally unraveled,
Leaving me raw and vulnerable.
For the first time,
A hug that gave me the calm of eternity,
A home where I could finally rest,
A hug that I squeeze a little tighter,
And hold a little longer,

Gripped by the haunting fear
Of how many months must pass
Before I can feel this again.
I surrender to the comfort it brings,
But the thought lingers, cruel and heavy
What if this is the last time I ever feel this?
The thought alone shatters my heart,
Filling me with painful, sleepless nights.
Touch -
The thing that keeps me alive,
The one thing I never knew I needed
Until it was finally given.

9. "A Love That Consumes"

This morning, the sunrise was different
A quiet revelation, soft as a sigh,
That the more resistance was forged on both sides,
The universe, in its vastness, shattered its boundaries
even further.
You can break through and deny love,
Dismiss care, chemistry, the dance of both joy and
sorrow,
But how does one escape the feeling of home
That warmth, that gentle embrace,
The only wish of the heart,
To freeze time, to hold that moment forever, unbroken?
There I was, as I always am, tangled in thoughts,
And slowly, his hands, like whispers of warmth,
Slipped around me, pulling me close,
His face buried in the tender curve of my neck.
In that sacred space, we spoke
We spoke of fear,
Of how we run from the very thing we've waited for all
our lives.

I was clumsy with my emotions,
Unskilled in how not to love him,
How to hold back a heart that only knew surrender.
I wanted to shout to the heavens:
"I've found my one, my soul's echo."
A gentle one, a love so soft and pure,
One I never thought I deserved.
There he stood, torn between heart and mind,
A battle so fierce, it turned into quiet indifference.
But none of that mattered,
Not my feelings, nor my wishes
All I wanted was for him to release the burden,
To trust me completely,
To know that I would never be a hindrance in his path,
That nothing would stand between him and his dreams,
And that this love was unconditional.
I whispered assurances, soft and certain,
That I was his—fully, irrevocably,
And that this love could not be undone.
He could love me freely, without fear,
And savor each moment,
Without the shadow of regret.
Isn't it better to have a love so pure,
So unmeasured, that it consumes you entirely,
Rather than to live without it at all?
This is my love
The love that wraps me in its fire and peace,

A love that holds me, completely,
As I surrender to its depth,
And in its embrace, I find my home.

10. "A Night Wrapped in Fire and Love"

A fresh, radiant day broke
Bright smiles, hearts full of promise,
We decided to let the day unfold,
To make memories and let the universe take its course.
We fought the urge to plan every detail,
And cast aside the perfect itinerary that never stood a
chance.
We danced, hands intertwined,
Laughter spilling from our souls,
Rolling on the soft grass, carefree and wild,
Meeting beautiful, strong women along the way,
Each encounter a fleeting but precious moment.
We climbed, our hearts light,
To a heavenly spot where a small shop served coffee and
simple delights.
In that place, we knew
This was the day's perfect twist,
A moment so right, it felt like fate.
As the night gently crept in, the air grew cooler,

And after hours of thrilling talks,
Of words that stirred the soul,
It was time for another dream to come true
A bonfire.
Little did I know,
This night would hold a magic all its own.
The fire crackled, its warm glow a beacon in the dark,
We circled around it, drinks in hand,
Our hearts open, our voices deep with connection.
With every passing second, the night grew more perfect,
More unforgettable, as if the world had paused just for
us.
As the evening wound down,
He gathered me into his embrace,
Laid his jacket on the grass like a bed of stars,
And pulled me close, my head resting on his chest.
There we lay, eyes turned to the sky,
Watching shooting stars tumble like fragments of
wishes,
As if the heavens themselves were celebrating with us.
He knew I'd longed to sleep under the stars,
But never imagined I'd find this moment with him.
With a heart so full, so overflowing,
The night ended with playful jumps and soft laughter.
And for once, he let go,
Letting his heart break free of all its walls.
No words were needed

His actions spoke louder than anything could.
In that silence, I heard it:
"You are mine."
And in that moment, I just knew!

11. "The Home I Never Knew"

Home... What is Home?
I grew up in a family,
Yet, I never knew home.
It was never safe,
Never soft enough to cradle my heart,
Never steady enough to still the storm in my mind.
Yes, I was shielded by walls,
But what is protection if it does not touch the soul?
Each time the world outside bruised me,
I had nowhere to run,
No place to curl up,
No quiet corner to inhale peace
Until the trembling in my chest finally stilled.
With the passing years,
The truth unfurled itself like a silent dawn
Home is not the house you occupy,
Nor the roof that shields your head.
Home is where the heart is held,
Where love anchors your spirit,

Where a person makes you whole.
I longed for a home without the echoes of rage,
Without the scream of blame splitting the air,
Without each tiny mistake etched like a scar,
Without doors that slammed like thunder,
And words that cut deeper than knives,
Words that made me question my very existence.
How can you call someone home
When they make you wonder
If you are merely a mistake of fate?
I wait
Yearning for a home,
Not of walls, but of warmth,
A refuge wrapped in tenderness,
Where peace blooms like a thousand flowers.
I dream of a home where fears vanish like smoke,
Where I am not only accepted,
But cherished
A home that claims me as its own,
Where my soul is no longer a wanderer,
But finds rest, at last, in the arms of belonging.

12. "Awakened by the Dark"

Where there is light,
there too resides darkness.
Haven't we all heard this before?
I truly believe in the magic that darkness holds
the power it possesses,
with its ability to unravel your life,
or, paradoxically, to illuminate it.
Yes, there can be no light without the shadow.
The allure of darkness consumes even the best of us,
yet it is only when we step into it,
drenched in its blackness,
that we truly come to cherish the brilliance of light,
as it beams, awakening life within each cell,
as if for the first time.
It is the void,
the emptiness,
that highlights the beauty of fullness.
So, the next time you find yourself lost,
remember: it is time to seek the light within.

13. "When Love Turns to Grief"

The loss of a loved one
is when love ignites,
a flame we never fully see
until it flickers out.
We are creatures of habit,
taking love for granted
the one who stands by you,
through every wound you've inflicted,
offering peace amidst your chaos,
and shelter in the storms of fear.
How often do we forget
the quiet power of their presence,
until one day
like a breath you never noticed
they're gone.
The silence they leave behind
is a weight that crushes the soul,
a panic rising from the deep,
wandering the streets in numb confusion,

trying to comprehend
the unbearable truth.
You awaken to a world
you wish were nothing more than a cruel dream,
gasping for air,
sobbing through the endless night,
yearning to feel their touch,
to hear their voice call your name.
It's been years since I've felt this ache,
this hollow longing
for someone who once filled every corner of my world.
Now, in the quiet of the night,
I find myself weeping at 3 a.m.,
haunted by the thought of losing them.
So, look around.
Hold them just a little tighter.
Breathe them in, and hold them close.
Let them feel your love,
for you never know how fleeting it may be.

14. "The Quiet Language of Love"

Experiencing love in its many forms,
I never truly knew which one reached deep within,
which one held the truest depth.
The glamour of fancy parties, date nights, and dinners
flowers and chocolates, sweet but fleeting,
just tender gestures without lasting meaning.
Until one day,
I caught myself smiling,
lost in the magic of his stories,
feeling a quiet excitement,
a warmth in the intimacy
of simply watching movies together,
every weekend,
side by side.
We understood each other so well
that our unspoken words
were enough to fill the spaces between us.
Taking spontaneous trips,
basking in the sunlight,

cuddling beneath a velvet sky,
the stars twinkling like secrets shared only with us.
And then, it became clear
my love language was conversation.
The deep, soul-stirring exchanges,
talking until the night folded into dawn,
sharing thoughts and dreams,
agreeing to disagree,
over a perfect cup of coffee.
The way our eyes met,
the smiles that lingered,
and in the silences that followed,
there was a peace
an unspoken contentment,
simply having each other,
breathing in those moments,
wrapped in the quiet beauty of being together.

15. "Mornings of Quiet Love"

The beauty of waking up together
surpasses all the beauty life has to offer.
The warmth of hands gently intertwined,
and the sense of home found in the shelter of his chest.
Eyes slowly opening,
gazing at the softness of his face,
deep in sleep,
lost in the quiet beauty of him.
In these moments, there is a love so profound,
a sacred stillness,
like the devotion of a Sufi soul,
whispered in the silence of morning light.
I wake him with soft pecks on his cheeks,
gentle kisses on his forehead,
whispering how much I treasure this moment,
and how I never want it to end.
The desire to stay wrapped in this warmth,
to linger in this sacred space,
or there is nothing more surreal,

nothing more heavenly,
than this love, untouched by time.
And as I lose myself in its purity,
his arms tighten around me,
matching my energy, my love,
speaking through his touch,
a silent promise: *I want this, too, forever.*

16. "Whispers of a Bookish Heart."

Books,
an escape from the painful grasp of reality,
In them, we endlessly search for lives,
for characters we long to meet in the world we know,
a longing we dare not voice aloud.
I call it the suspension of reality
where you live the lives you cannot claim,
inhale the scent of fresh pages,
as you annotate your thoughts in the margins,
like two friends whispering their deepest secrets,
unraveling their darkest fears,
words stained with tears,
or a smile that betrays the heart's joy,
with every romance that lingers long after the last page.
And then, the thrill of a murder mystery
each twist a pulse that quickens your breath,
the sharp edges of suspense cutting deep into your mind,
until every theory shatters,
and you're left tangled in the aftermath,

mind reeling from the brilliant puzzle,
unable to untangle the final threads.
By the time the book closes,
you press it close to your chest,
and for a moment,
you are submerged in a serenity
a peaceful stillness that is only yours,
a treasure shared quietly between you and the pages,
a secret the world will never know,
an intimacy only you own,
the story, bound forever between you and the book.

17. "A Symphony of Friendship and Strength"

What is more special,
more magnificent than the bond of family?
It's the books we immerse ourselves in,
the worlds we believe in,
where every page whispers a piece of our soul.
It's that woman who, with every glance,
reminds you of your strength,
the best friend who never fails to see
the beauty that resides within you
both in spirit and in form.
It's the wild-hearted woman,
always chasing adventure,
lost in chaotic horror tales
that stir the depths of her being,
and the loyal friend who listens
to the endless, whimsical chatter,
the secrets shared between only the two of you.
And her - oh, her!
An embodiment of unwavering strength,

with a heart so vast,
its love knows no bounds,
always nurturing mine,
lifting it higher,
without asking for anything in return.
The truth I'm trying to say is this
the one chance life grants us,
the one gift God offers,
to build a family of our own,
lies in the friendships we hold close.
Friendships that are pure,
honest, and a little wild
a home away from home,
where our hearts find refuge.
And oh, how deeply,
how profoundly,
I love them.

18. "Moonlit Souls: The Dance of Divine Feminine"

Did you know,
the moon's cycles are intricately tied to the rhythm of
girls?
There's something uniquely magical about them,
like angels whispering secrets to the stars,
sharing their energy with the moon in a dance no one
else can understand.
They are the mystical witches,
destined to twirl in enchanted forests,
like free-spirited birds with wings of light,
soaring effortlessly beneath the velvet sky.
The light they carry is more radiant than the moon itself
a glow that kisses the world with wonder.
When the full moon's energy meets theirs,
it's a celestial ballet,
as the universe aligns in awe of the most powerful force
the feminine energy, unstoppable and infinite.
Such women are not bound by the world's expectations,
they were born to break every chain,

and dance freely in the winds of their own destiny.
They are flames of fire,
untamed and fierce
and only a soul of equal brilliance can stand beside them.
They are the ones who fear change the most,
yet, in the end, they are the very ones who reshape the
world with grace.
She is the human form of the moon
gentle, pure, and endlessly honest,
her light shining in the darkness,
gently guiding all who wander.
Like the moon, she gives her brilliance to everything
around her,
even if it means fading just a little,
to warm the cold night with her glow,
for every heart that looks up to her.
She is love, she is grace,
smiling softly amidst the storms,
the quiet strength in every rumble of the world.
She is the moon
a constant reminder that even in the darkest hours,
light and beauty always find their way.

19. "The Silent Agony of Unrequited Love"

Love is powerful,
isn't it?
When she loves you,
she loves you like a storm
wild and uncontained,
like an abandoned house finding its family,
like a lost bird returning to its nest.
She loves you like the sun loves the sky
like you were the first and only soul to ever be loved.
Her love knows no limits,
it's boundless,
unwritten,
selfless.
She'll dance in your darkness,
turn your flaws into beauty,
and stand beside you, no questions asked,
ready to partner in your most reckless dreams.
But still,
is it enough?

Is it still powerful enough?
Her love is pure
pure enough to bring you to your knees,
to cradle you in arms that heal the deepest scars,
that unravel generations of pain
and turn wounds into wisdom.
Her love fades the marks of time
and wraps warmth around the coldest corners of your
soul.
Yet the question remains:
Is it enough?
Is it powerful enough to reach the places it should?
She gives and gives,
her heart overflowing with all the love the world can
hold,
but he, the one who's longed for it,
is like a tsunami crashing into a sea of calm,
a fire she must walk through,
only to be burned by the endless waves of love
that never seem to touch him.
He won't feel a thing.
He runs from the warmth,
inflicting pain on himself,
sabotaging the very beauty the universe has given him.
No matter how much she loves,
no matter how much she sacrifices,
her love remains powerless

a song with no echo
for the one who refuses to hear it,
for the one who does not know how to receive it.
And in that silence,
her love
so pure, so vast
remains a beautiful tear
never reaching the heart that needed it most.

20. "The Art of Never Letting Go"

In a world where voices echo,
preaching the art of letting go,
where ego and respect are measured in love's name,
I say, **don't.**
Don't let go.
When you love with a fire that ignites your soul,
when it's true, when it's pure,
when it's as honest as the sky's first light
you fight.
You fight with every breath,
until time itself stands still,
for it's only love that's worth fighting for.
How hollow would your heart be
if there was nothing left to stand for?
How could you know forever
without the strength to hold hands tighter,
to endure the storms that rage around you?
How could you face the world's cruelty
without a heart forged in power,

unbroken, steadfast?
It's not in letting go
that life finds its meaning
it's in the art of holding on.
Hold on when the world whispers to walk away,
when every trial pulls at your seams.
Add fire to your spirit.
Be the one who stays,
the one who nourishes love with resilience,
who breathes life back into it,
even when the world says it's easier to leave.
For in the end, it is **your fight**
that makes love eternal
your courage, your strength,
the love you refuse to let fade.

21. "Reborn in the Stillness of Falling Snow"

It's as if his presence
illuminates the world,
recharging the very universe in my favor.
Every time we unite,
the world dances to the rhythm of my heartbeat,
and everything falls into place,
as though the stars themselves are aligning just for us.
For years, I longed for snowfall,
dreamed of it, planned for it,
but somehow, it always slipped away.
Then, in his presence,
with no expectations,
he spoke with a calmness that made everything seem
possible:
"Just be in the moment.
Everything will fall into place."
With his unwavering confidence,
I let go, placing all my faith in him.
How could I not?

I smiled, no longer concerned about whether the snow
would fall.
All I wanted was to embrace the moment,
to cherish the time we had,
without letting my past fears ruin it,
like they had every other time.
I took a deep breath,
feeling the crisp air fill my lungs,
and stepped outside into the silence of the world,
the mountains standing tall and beautiful,
the air biting, pure, and cold.
And then
the most unexpected and beautiful thing happened.
The snow began to fall.
There it was
my greatest dream,
right before me,
like a gift from the heaven.
Tears welled up,
but I couldn't stop smiling,
looking up at the sky,
astonished by what was unfolding.
In that moment, I realized
I had fallen in love with life.
I had fallen in love with the person standing beside me,
and with every little thing that made this moment so
perfect.

For once, it was *my* world,

and it was all mine.

The biggest change?

I felt an overwhelming gratitude for being alive.

For the simple, precious act of breathing,

for the gift of this day,

for the chance to witness something beautiful,

something I once thought I'd never be able to experience.

His words echoed softly,

like a whisper in the wind:

"God must be proud today,

to have made you happy, just for once."

It was as if he had seen the deepest part of my soul,

and understood that all I ever wanted was peace,

that every day had once been a battle I was too tired to

fight.

But now

now, in this moment,

I realized how much I had been missing.

For the first time, I felt alive.

I wasn't just surviving,

I was truly living.

And in that moment of snow falling softly around me,

I finally understood that life,

in all its messiness and beauty,

was worth it.

For once, I didn't wish for an end.

I was grateful for this breath,
this life,
this *moment.*
I had once lost sight of everything
lost in the darkness of despair,
not knowing how to escape it.
But now, in the light of this snow,
I found something I never thought I'd see again:
hope.
I found myself.
And for the first time in forever,
I wasn't just existing -I was living.
I was enough.
And that was enough.